NO BULLSH** GUIDE TO GETTING A JOB

WHAT THEY DON'T WANT YOU TO KNOW

How to build a resume, find a job and interview like a champ.

JASON LEBLANC

NO BULLSH** GUIDE TO GETTING A JOB
Published by Jason LeBlanc with the help of Lulu.com. 9572
Desert Willow Way, Highlands Ranch CO 80129

ISBN: 978-0-6151-7083-1

This publication is designed to provide a process of finding a job
and interviewing for it. The subject matter, strategies and
processes are based on the personal successes of the author. It is
sold with the understanding that the publisher nor author is not
engaged rendering legal, accounting, or other professional
service. If legal advice or other expert assistance is required, the
services of a competent professional should be sought. Also, the
author is speaking about his experiences and would not suggest
that anyone who is uncomfortable with his thoughts or ideas to
implement them.

For additional copies please visit Lulu.com.

CONTENTS

FOREWORD

In memory of my father, Claude Finis LeBlanc, who was equal parts dreamer and lover of mankind. Thanks for letting me learn on my own but always being a nonhypocritical and honest role model. You were right; I had to graduate from the "School of hard knocks". I'll see you soon…don't catch all the big fish up there, save some for me!

For my mother, Dad was the luckiest man on earth and he knew it. You are beautiful and incredible. Thank you for your unconditional love, selflessness and support. You are truly unique…I love you!

Thank you to my lovely and supportive wife Heather. She is my soul mate and inspiration to write this book. She spent many nights tirelessly helping me to get the words out. I love you Vixxen.

WHAT NO BULLSH** GUIDE TO GETTING A JOB IS ALL ABOUT

I am here to share with you how to build a resume, find a job and interview like a champ. The information you will find in this book is not taught; it is reality, shaped and channeled to attain results fast. All that is mentioned is based on factual experiences of a job getting Sensei, me. If you need proof, I have defeated over 100 interviewers and accepted 28 of those jobs by the age of 30. These weren't all in the same field either. They range from finance, banking, sales (clients, transactional, retail, business to business,) homebuilding, management, warehouse, physical labor, research, hospitality, hospitals and even self-employment. My main driver was and is money.

I wanted to know how to keep getting more money from each job. Ancillary to that is the fact that I have had an interest in many different careers. Follow the techniques in this book and you too can achieve financial success at the job of your dreams. The underlying theme of this book and the concept you need to take home is that it's you against them. "Them" is management. Don't worry about your competition.

The most important piece to the job getting puzzle is the interview, where it is all about you. At least what you tell them and what they can prove. You will learn many techniques I have discovered on my journey. Namely, how to thwart the system and learn how the hiring process works. Getting a job is all about understanding the hiring processes within the system and how you can use it as a tool. Instead of feeling like one when you don't get the job.

Everyone will go through some variation of system. So know that I am a warrior who has been on the front lines with all of you for years and you will find value in this book. As many of my friends have when I helped them land their choice jobs. It is through their collective urging that I write this book to help all of you.

This book is a powerful tool for you to use. It is purposely doubled spaced in order to allow you to write notes, thoughts and ideas in the margins. I organized it to take you from thinking about a career, making your first move by building a resume, finding a job, interviewing and finally, landing the job. If you heed my advice and relentlessly pursue your goals, the world will be your oyster.

This book, if used as a guide on your journey, will navigate you through the tough realm of the elusive job. I only hesitate to say it will absolutely work for everyone, because I don't want to get sued; but it works for me. The only other disclaimer I will make for the rest of this book is that these techniques aren't necessarily the way to get a job as deemed by society- but it sure is the most effective. It is a battle waged in gray area not a pack of lies. You will need to harness that gray area and perfect your story. The very best actors get it down pat with hard work and rehearsing. I'm sure your like everyone else on this planet and would like to have been a movie star, hell me too. Here is your chance to act, live, as often as you like. Trust me, even the toughest opponents fall. It does not matter if they are a small Mom and Popshop or a multinational corporation worth billions. It is all the same so don't be afraid just read on. Spread the word and help your friends- unless they are vying for the same job!

QUESTIONS TO ASK YOURSELF WHEN THINKING

ABOUT WHAT JOB YOU WANT

"Choices, choices, choices" so they say in college, or lack thereof it seems in reality. What is a person to do? What job do you take? What career should you pursue? You don't want to waste time and you don't want to be poor. You finally come to terms with the fact that unless you're a trust fund baby or have connections through friends and family—no job is going to buzz you at 10:30 a.m. No one will say " Hey, I need you, you are so different than the other employees – I can tell. You have a ton to offer my multimillion-dollar company and me. Come on please get up, we all get along so well, and you can make some dough here. You will move right up to the top. Whaddya say…"

10:29a.m. You wake up from this dream one minute before your real alarm goes off.

This chapter is about giving life to an idea or thought. So you don't end up alone asking yourself "What to do today?"

The first question you must ask yourself is "Where do I want to end up?"

When you sit back and reflect on your long successful life, what would you really rather think? Did you pass up any opportunities? Do you have any real regrets? Did you sculpt your life or just fit into the mold of others? Did you ever break out of your own mold and go after it? Did you set a goal and feel the joy of pursuing it relentlessly until you accomplished it, then reveled in it?

You must start at the end of your journey and work your way back to the beginning. This will create the momentum necessary to drive you through life. Visualize each step along the way and never be concerned about improvising, changing or working in the gray.

It is okay to dream here- in fact that would be a stronger exercise. If you set a gargantuan goal then you will more than likely to accomplish a large goal. Shoot for the moon and land amongst the stars is another way to put it. Look at problems, changes and the unknown as challenges not roadblocks. Most importantly, don't worry about others and their opinions. You just do what you have to do within legal and moral limits.

Next question: Do you follow the money or your dreams? Is it possible to do both?

You have to be true to your core on this one. No one is around, what do you think? Would you rather have the creative freedoms or create your own financial freedom. Do you want to really enjoy your job, so much that you would do it for damn near free, perhaps living paycheck to paycheck and have creative freedom? Or, would you sacrifice that for budgeting your money, making it work for you through investments and be prepared for retirement with plenty of dough around. The benefit of a corporate job is that you pretty much do what you want outside of work, therefore creating a different freedom. It is almost like you have to buy it from the corporations and the government. You must use them as tools instead of the other way around. Make money and prestige in the corporate world, but set a monetary retirement goal and use the corporations to make that happen. Play by their rules and try to enjoy the game. Then, if you think you are strong enough, go do your own thing. Leave the security of the corporation and its stable. Leave, lay it on the line and have faith that you can make your dreams happen.

Be courageous. Maybe you can make enough to follow your passion, create your freedom and financial success. Time is on your side if you see your finances as a process, develop a plan and take a step forward. It is better to follow through and complete your goal, and move on to the next one. Try not to change your goal all the time. It would cause paralysis of action and loss of any current momentum attained.

It is definitely possible to follow your dreams and the money. It's a process and a relentless commitment. Lady Fortune is a wonderful chance occurrence that can make great things happen for those she blindly lands on. For the rest of us, we constantly need to have our eyes open and fingers on the pulse, prepared for and pursuing goals. So we must readily recognize and capitalize on any given moment seizing the opportunity when it presents itself. Think of it as action causes reaction. It does not matter what you are pursuing or working on. The point is, you are doing it rather than thinking about it. You thereby dramatically increase the propensity for opportunities to happen, you don't have to be super perfectionist Ben Franklin but you don't want to be Rip Van Winkle either. There is a happy medium for each person to find, think about Kris Christopherson. Not that he is the most well known example I can think of. Nor do I listen to his music or think much of him as an actor. But he certainly exhibits my example best. What he is to me, is a goal setting man with relentless commitment who is a perfect example of what I'm trying to get across to you.

The man was a military guy in his youth. He flew helicopters, but he always had an interest in poetry and writing music. Upon fulfilling his military commitment he was about to take a job at WestPoint teaching English. He decided to chuck it all and go work entry level in a Nashville recording studio. I mean low entry. He would empty ashtrays, toss garbage, and empty drinks. Then one day, he met Johnny cash. Kris wanted so badly for Johnny to read and hear his songs that he pursued him relentlessly. He even flew a chopper to Johnny's home! Albeit, it does not always take such a grandiose idea, just a creative one. After some time, Johnny invited Kris onto his show; the rest is sweet history for Kris. He even became an actor; who knew "Whistler" from the film Blade could sing?

Question three: Should I stay or should I go? If I go, is it for the place or the job?

This question really depends on three variables:

1) What type of job you are getting.

2) Your history/reputation in the town.

3) Should you be committed to quality of life or pursuit of money?

If you have a good reputation and no criminal record you are off to a good start. If people know whom you and like you, then stay in town. I say this, if you do not desire to be in a different place nor do you mind passing up better opportunities). The trade off is stability and familiarity, above all, you feel good being there. But I will say this, if you desire to be in a different place, pursue it. New places offer different and often better opportunities. It can be exhilarating and rejuvenating. As you explore the town, scene, people and activities.

Finance, banking, any sales and management are all based on building and maintaining relationships. It never cuts off. If you want to stay in town I would ask yourself one question; " Do I have any connections here for sustainable business?" If "No", look at a different line of work or jet. If "Yes" then no worries. If you are in any other field, you get a free ride as long as you have the credentials. In other words, you do not rely on relationships to get paid; you just have to work. Downside is that you might have to leave against your will if there is no work in your field. But that evens out your free ride in terms of a relocation package.

If you decide to jet for the job and handle it, then embrace the change; absolutely do it. Because you can always move back, and you never truly know something until you feel it and try it. Not to mention that there is one undeniable truth in jobs, the more responsibility you take on the more you will get paid. That is to say always be looking for opportunity to increase your responsibility. I would suggest trying it out for six months to see if you take to the change. Go cheap while you are there, budget your money, get a cheap place and go absorb the culture. If you own a home, I would lease it for at least six months. In three months you will just be getting a handle on things. In six months you will be moving and grooving and it's either working or it's not. No need to hold out another year, your feelings won't change.

There is something to be said for jetting. It enables you to be a different person, create a new life and have new experiences. This very much relates to getting a job because people will not know you. They only know what you tell them and they will only research so much on you. This is an advantage and a trump card if you know how to play your hand while keeping a good poker face. This essentially allows you to sculpt your story to your liking. Nothing is more important than getting your story down cold and make sure it's seamless. It is not that you have something to hide. You are presenting the stylized and best view of yourself possible. This is the spotlight, so sing your bloody arse off.

You can certainly apply this strategy in your hometown but be careful not to trip up due to the congruency of your story combined with public knowledge. You will instead need to give your story a light rub with no extra sauce. It only takes one misinterpretation to throw you off, or, one friend of a friend. Do not spice up, use your actual degrees and/or licensing. Apply this to any job or experience where the employer knows someone they can verify with. I don't mean human resources, I mean someone that knows you and/or them personally.

Should I go to college, get a masters, go to trade school or f** it all?

Recall I am thirty years old and in my Generation-X, our parents probably did not go to college, especially in the South where I'm from. It was not this way for my generation. While I was a kid the option of just going to high school already was fading. Your opportunities were measurably decreasing. By the time I reached the college age of 18, the paradigm shifted again. It became clear that you were going have to go to college if you wanted any opportunity. You could still pursue trades like plumbing and contracting making good money. Busting your back until you grow enough to hire people for you. This path means you need to be intrinsically motivated and responsible enough to run your own show. There became an intermediate between the options of high school and college, trade schools.

Many people decided to go this route. It is less time, on average two years, less money and you get specific job training on technology, medical, law, etc. These alternatives are usually great careers with solid opportunity.

In the time it took me to leave college and Generation Y was bucking up, I noticed another shift in the paradigm. There was a decreasing amount of opportunities available to recent graduates. It seems the market was saturated. Not a doomsday affair, but measurable decreases. Competition was getting even tougher.

It became apparent to me that the norm of having to go to college soon evolved into having to go to graduate school. A tough option if you do not have a scholarship. You have just spent four to six years and a ton of dough. Getting a Bachelor's in "not enough". Now you must commit to another two to four years and fork over a ton of more dough to go to graduate school. But even now that level of schooling is starting to mean less. You are still more marketable if you have gone to graduate school, but the affect on opportunities is measurably less than it was five years ago. I suppose the next natural shift in the paradigm will be attaining a PhD, whose value seems to be losing ground. For now competition, competition, competition. It will not decrease, only grow and get tougher. You can survive and beat the odds. Make a decision, form a plan and execute it. Be sure to measure your progress along the way. Make that first step and the rest will assuredly be easier to deal with.

As far as f** it all- unless you want to turn to crime or move to Panama your only other option is welfare and the dependence on the kindness of others.

RESUME

Your resume is a funny thing. It must simultaneously blend standard, easy formatting that is easy to read and still must stand out from the others. Once you give it life you can then make it a soldier. Relentlessly pursuing opportunity by downloading it to two to three online headhunters like Monster, Career builder and your local newspaper. Hopefully they have a web presence, if not you might want to think about jetting. After a couple of hours of inputting your information, you now have a soldier in the form of a search engine that you can send out on many different missions. With this you can search for different career opportunities simultaneously in multiple cities every day.

If you don't want to spend the time searching, you can still input your information give it a good title and let the employers look for you. A good title speaks of experience and in as few words as possible. No big words, just simple like " Five years mortgage experience, knowledge of all loans". Remember the employer/recruiter is glazing over hundreds of resumes a day. Try to be creative but not too loud.

The employer/recruiter will contact you through email or phone, whichever you indicate. I suggest the cell phone, that way you never miss a call. If you can't talk at that moment you can always call back in a few minutes. I try not let it go to voicemail if I can help it. Employers and recruiters like to get you on the first try. It would be helpful to answer your phone as "Hello, this is ____." Also, have a more professional voicemail. Not too cool, no music, not silly and not flat, " Hello, this is ___-, I can't come to the phone right now, but leave a message and I 'll call you back shortly, thanks." Another tidbit is to fax and email your resume if given both options by the employer.

How do you make your resume easy to read while making it stand out from the others?

You should format your resume in such a way that it fills one page. I do mean one and only one page. If you do not have enough experience to fill a page then you better come up with some other relevant information about you. For example, you could have a section on computer skills, hardware, software and relevant classes. You can also include honors and clubs. Do not include an activity or hobby section. For instance, if you mountain bike then you could belong to a bike club. Unless you are applying in the South, I would not mention that you belong to a gun club. Label this section "Community Involvement". I will expound on what to do with this information during an interview later. The format of the resume should flow smoothly and clearly from job title, and be bullet point your job duties and functions directly under the title. Another addition you can make is to elaborate and /or separate your duties and functions. Be very descriptive, using sentences beginning with an action words like "Performed" or "Responsible for". Be sure to separate the duties and functions from each other; do not combine any. Bullet point the action words in one to two line sentences (preferably one line) and list at least three different line items of your duties or functions under each bullet. (See Format next page.) Also, you can always elongate your objective; but be careful not to run on and sound overblown. This is the first thing an employer/recruiter reads after your name and location. It is most important to make a solid great first impression.

If you have too much experience, too many clubs or community involvement, it would be best to highlight the majors. For example, you could reduce your computer skills section by losing the hardware and just mention a few relevant, (meaning people still use it) programs. You can dramatically reduce your relevant courses or just lose them altogether. You could also reduce your objective, and use smaller font.

Font sizing, spacing and margin placement can be your worst enemy or your best friend when you are trying to put together your resume. This process can take thirty minutes to two hours depending on you. Use your formatting tools to your advantage whether you need to fill up the page because you do not have enough information, or if you need more space because you have a lot of information to put down. For example, if you need more space, then decrease the margins both top, bottom and side to side. Reduce your font size in between your sentences to impact line spacing. In other words, if you are using a twelve font size (which I recommend) make the blank line in between sentences a ten font size or eight. You place your name at the top of the page. Bold it, do not italicize or go too big maybe fourteen but not more than sixteen on the font size. Next you should enter your address and phone number on the same line. The third line should be your email address. Whatever you do, do not hyperlink it. It will not print out well. You should center these lines on the page and then place a thin to medium black line across the page from left to right.

Next you have the <u>Objective</u> statement. Make it to the point simple; yet eloquent. A great example of an Objective would be " to acquire a challenging position, utilizing skills developed through my work experience and education with the opportunity for professional growth based upon performance." Do not worry about asserting your personality or being different here.

Beneath the <u>Objective</u> statement place any licensing or internships. Some might argue to not place internships here, rather later under education or as work experience. You make the call. If you do place something here, align the dates in the right hand margin on the same line. For example License: Series 7, October 2006. Bold the whole line and use the date you attained the license.

The next line is <u>Experience</u>; if you don't have any then you do not pass go. As an alternative, you can use your education instead. There is nothing wrong with that option, but remember this book is about making you the most marketable possible. My advice is to list any job, and include at least one on your resume. Also tenure looks strong on a resume. Having a job for two years looks good. Listing two to three jobs is okay, but not four or more. That destroys the stability factor that employers and recruiters are concerned about. If you stay at one job for two years or more years you're considered a stable and consistent employee. You are worth spending money on training and being apart of the club.

On the same line as <u>Experience</u>, place the position title and underline it. Next list the company name, city and state then month and year. Everything is bolded except the city and state and make all of it fit on one line. Your dates need to be on the same line but aligned along the right side of the page. For example,

Position Title, Company name, City, State   *start date- End date or "Present"*

Bullet point underneath Job title and list each duty or function. Each duty should be ideally be on one line and no more than two. Start with action words. Do not be afraid to elaborate and perfect your story. For example, if you were in some kind of sales you could make several bullet points saying, " Promoted and sold product/service", "Conducted group presentations", " Created solutions for product/service" and "Established relationships through cold calling". Be sure to bullet point each.

Feel free to add customer service numbers like "attained a 92% customer satisfaction rate for two consecutive quarters". Remember, the burden of proof in on them.

I will elaborate on how to answer these sometimes awkward questions in the interview chapter. If you have management experience, then be sure to build on that. Perhaps instead of three people underneath you, you managed seven to ten. Do not put a number on the resume but be prepared for the question in the interview.

If you ran your own business then expound upon the many duties and tasks you preformed. "Conducted business as a sole proprietor executing all business decisions and accounting

23

work". Another way to say it would be "Performed all administrative duties". "Responsible for originating business", "Managed all third party and client relationships". You can even sculpt that you conducted sales trainings and that you managed X amount of people who you hired. No one knows how your business was conducted dig.

Also, place under Experience if you were a graduate school assistant or a similar program in college or tech school. Use the same format, dates and all. One important point about using this option is, do not overcomplicate this section. If you were doing some real heady work then boil it down. Use layman terms and as few words as possible. Imagine explaining this to your grandma or some kid.

If you were in the military, God bless and thank you. This is a wonderful thing to have on resumes. Employers /recruiters really like military or don't, there is no in-between. What they usually like is heady part of it, like computer, satellite or communications. They also like medical and management. They do not seem to prefer the Dragon Gunner or Anti Tank Assault. They certainly don't want to know that you handled demolitions and plastic explosives. This is cool when your out talking with your friends and telling stories or even watching it on TV. Not so cool in an interview and certainly not on a

24

resume. You will scare the piss out of them. You are probably a cool person but they will not know that until they meet you and they certainly will not know it through your resume. The goal here would be to soften it up a bit. For example, as a job title you might put Squad Leader and then follow the same format as other jobs. Something like "Led Marines through combat exercise "is good. It shows leadership, responsibility and that you follow orders. Harking back to my explosives example, I would instead say "Responsible for training Marines on safety procedures".

If you have only worked manual labor jobs, then you need to talk about the number of projects you did, or some sort of measurement. "Worked in a warehouse and filled X amount of orders a day", " Responsible for inventory controls". With outside labor it is the same idea. Try to elaborate more on managing the project and/or people. If you cut grass and the boss would leave the site during the day and left you as the go to man, then there you have it. You "Managed a project and /or people". One important note, do your best to never leave a job on bad terms. Be sure that you have a decent relationship with your boss and /or the person who would be talking to any employer/recruiter that calls them. This does not take a whole lot of work. Be somewhat pleasant and think about how someone might respond to what you are going to say before you say it. This will be the cornerstone of the interview chapter.

Now that you have Experience mastered, let's take a look at the Education section. Bold **Education** and have it line up on the left hand margin under Experience. On this same line under Job Titles, place name of school attended and bold it as well as city and state. Below this, place ***Graduation*** (italicize and bold it), then the month and year. Below that, place ***Degree*** (italicize and bold it), list degree or degrees. If you have a high GPA (3.5 or above) then put it here. If not, then don't put anything. If you received any scholarships then place them on the next line. Graduate school or any other higher education goes before college. You always want the most recent items first. You should add computer skills on another line Next line you list Awards and/or Honors. The following line is for related coursework. If you are not just putting in names of courses then bullet point in order to describe the coursework. This is a better way to go.

The last thing you should list on this new beautiful one page resume is **"References furnished upon request".** This should be bolded and centered on the page. This is important to place on the resume because it says you have the references, and yet are not wasting their time or money on extra paper to read. It also buys you time to secure the right references if you do not already have them. Besides, the employer/recruiter does not usually care. Its probably 25/75 that they ask to see them. If they do, it is usually once you have interviewed and they want to hire you.

You will then be asked to write three names down on the application. Again, 25/75 if they actually call the references, but I would be prepared. Have one separate sheet with three names of people who will say something great about you. It is not necessary for them to have been your boss, could be a co-worker/friend. Try not to use family and if you use your girlfriend/ boyfriend or whatever; make sure you have your story straight. I would not mention the relationship, say they are a co-worker or old friend. You need to have their occupation, phone number, address, years known, what they are to you. Again, you only need three people, who preferably have known you for at least two years or will say they have.

Now would be a good time to address what employers/recruiters are looking for in a resume. There are a few over arching themes that they prefer such as leadership. Also, they look for tenure of at least one year at a job, but two years or more works even better. They want to see awards, project or service goals, management and a steady progression. They want to see you are educated, have direction and that your job or history has strong relevance to what they are hiring for. Most importantly they look for congruency.

So how do we communicate and display this persona and make it an extension of who we are?

To display leadership look to our military, management or grass cutting job. In these positions you have been in charge somehow someway in the past or present.

To reflect tenure, round of to the nearest year if possible. If you have received awards use them. For project or service goals simply use the ones you have in place at your job. If there aren't any in place, then create them. Nine times out of ten the employer /recruiter will not make you verify it. Now don't get to crazy. If you have metrics in place then follow those. Don't be worried if you recall different numbers than what is on file. For management, remember that even one day running the show still counts. You don't have to volunteer how long you did it for.

Having a steady direction means that you are always moving up even by switching jobs or changing careers. You can get away with this a lot between the ages of 16-24, after that you need to space it out a couple of years or have a great explanation. We will cover this more in the interview chapter.

For education, it is okay if it is not college, graduate school or tech school. The point is to display that you can be taught and trained. Having direction is simply your objective statement. It is saying that you set goals. As for the history and relevance, well, this should be obvious. While it is okay that you apply for jobs that you have not done before, just be sure to have some relation to it on your resume. Once you get the interview you can have a great answer and tie it together for them.

Congruency, I love that word, it makes things work together and flow. That is exactly what we want to accomplish with your resume. Flow will make you look strong. It also means you have tenure dates back to back. Your jobs and resume must make sense and

it must have a good format. It shows that you care enough and are smart enough to put together a top shelf resume, one that displays initiative.

I would like to take a moment and boil the resume process down to a few concepts that I want y'all to chew on. Also note that I will elaborate on what happens to your resume and what is verified later in the human resources section. Here are a couple of tidbits to digest and use to you advantage at this stage of the game. Realize that no one reading your resume is going to call anyone on it or verify anything. They will only get turned on and call you or not. It is up to you to interview properly. That is the juice of getting a job and the art that you will learn from me. We will delve into that in the next chapter.

One other note is that you need to always send your resume with a cover letter. Whether emailed, faxed or dropped off. The cover letter should look exactly like the top portion of your resume. Name, home address, phone number, email and the infamous black line traversing the page.

Below it you should include the date on the left. If you are faxing or emailing heavily then you can leave the date off so that you don't have to reprint it everyday. Below that you should have three to eight sentences, no more than a paragraph is my standard. Say something simple, professional positive and personal. For example:

"To whom it may concern:
I thought you may have an interest in my qualifications for a position within your company. I have enclosed my resume for y our review and approval. I would like to schedule a personal inte rview where we can discuss my enthusiasm for a position within your organization. I can be reached at the email address or telep hone number listed above. Thank you for your time and

consideration. I look forward to hearing from you soon.

Best regards,

Be sure to sign your name between the "Best regards" salutation and "your name".

Place the title of the position after "for a_____position " and place the company name after "within _____". If you are sending out a lot of resumes then leave it to save time and printing. A clever cover letter and congruent resume will provide a tight package to sell your product.

  Shifting back to the resume, recall that this resume is to be simple, straightforward and easy to read. Using few words as possible. You may be wondering, "What's so different?". The difference is that you are not the only one with a fantastic resume; many other people have taken my advice. But you are separating yourself from the herd that has resumes that are too long or short. They may be very hard to read because of funky font that is too large or small. Their resumes are not easy on the eyes and spaced or bolded incorrectly. They have bad formatting or bad phone numbers. They are not up to date or they do not know how to describe what they do. More so, they do not know themselves or how to engage a person through a resume. While writing your resume you are learning who you are and what you do. You have got your story down cold –with a little spice to make it nice. Furthermore, you are learning how to engage a employer/recruiter through a written format so that they get to know who you are. They will take notice of you and your resume in the way you want to be noticed-professional and solid. Don't worry your resume will always stand out by combining all that I have mentioned with who you are. You are sculpting your story as how only you can tell. There is no one else like you so no two stories will be the same. I am sharing knowledge with you that I have gained while traveling on the same path you are on now. Use my knowledge as a resource and my tidbits as tools. Understand my concepts to make yourself as strong as possible. In short, learn my techniques for your life sculpture. Are you ready for the Juice? Then lets move to the next chapter to learn some bombastic interview techniques so that you can prepare for your performance and nail it cold every time.

YOUR NAME
Your Address, Your cell
Your email address

OBJECTIVE:
To acquire a challenging position, utilizing skills developed
through my education and work experience with the opportunity
for professional growth based on performance.

LICENSE: Type and License #   Month, Year

EXPERIENCE:
Title of job, Name of Company, City, State   Month, Year

- Originated Loans through relationship with X company.
- Managed Client base consisting of x amount.
- Worked as part of a team who achieved all company
  goals.

Title of job, Name of Company, City, State   Month, Year
- Originated product by establishing relationships and cold
  calling.
- Managed all client and third party relationships.
- Conducted business as a sole proprietor.

Title of job, Name of Company, City, State   Month, Year
- Led all company sales efforts and all methods of
  prospecting.
- Conducted sales training for new employees.
- Created proposals and company marketing material.
- Provided solutions to clients for x type of work.

EDUCATION:
University, City, State
Graduation:
Degree: Minors: GPA
Awards and Honors:
Computer Skills:
Related Courses:

References Provided Upon Request
**** This is a great format and remember to use action words to
begin your sentences.

33

THE INTERVIEW

If you have executed what I have taught you with your resume and you made it this far, guess what? You are halfway there. No kidding. You are about to face the toughest and most demanding part of getting the job; the Interview. Make no bones about it this is where you are made or broken. It is here that you seal the deal and put on your show about your life. Who you are and your work history. This is not a place for the weak of wills. You will have nothing to fear if you have prepared your story and you have it cold. This way you can focus on your nonverbal communication. Upon mastering both of these skills you will present yourself in the absolute best possible light. Remember, nothing is more important than coming across as genuine.

At this point, you have given serious thought about the direction of your life. You have also accomplished two skills. The first, learning how to prepare through self-reflection. Then, through resume writing you have now learned how to project yourself on paper. Now you are ready to study the art of the interview. You will learn the skill of performing (some may call it acting). Call it what you will, if you don't nail this part you are not in the movie, dig?

The interview has three main components: the greeting, the information exchange (probing) and the close. When you show up for the interview always, always, always wear a suit, always be 15 minutes early, and always bring at least five resumes with you. You really only need one or two in the interview but be prepared and have five at any give time. You never know, you might need to interview with several people, sometimes the interviewer does not have a legible copy or are able to locate their copy of your resume. Besides, it makes you look like you cover all the angles and you get to exhibit this by providing something for the interviewer proactively. Also, bring your license, social security card and a blank check that's voided before you leave the house. If things progress rapidly you will need all this. If not, at least you are prepared.

The suit should go without saying; there is nothing wrong with being the best-dressed person in the room. It shows pride, professionalism and seriousness about the job. At this moment I am literally having my wife sit down and write on how to dress. She is a young professional with a national homebuilder.

For men, dressing is easier. Start with the pin strip dark suit. A crisp white shirt is always the best choice. For your tie, choice a solid colored sateen fabric in silver or gold. These ties look conservative, clean, and subtly eye catching. Also, French cuffs and cuff links are a classy touch. Freshly polished black shoes, preferably patent leather, are a must. Polished shoes are just that, polished. Be well groomed and cut your hair shorter then your neckband. It makes you look more professional and mature.

Women have a more options, but I still recommend a suit. Pants or a knee length skirt is acceptable, but always make sure you are topping it off with a blazer. A blouse of a neutral color is appropriate, stay away from loud colors or dressing head to toe in black. If you are wearing a skirt, always wear hose. Closed round-toed heels or a modest loafer does the trick. Pull your hair back in a low ponytail or a loose bun. In most interviews sex does not sell. Your look needs to be closer to schoolteacher than sexpot. Finish off your outfit with pearls or diamond studs.

Always arrive fifteen minutes early. This will make you shine; anything will help. If you are one minute late, you will make a bad impression that you now have to overcome.

So do yourself the favor look up the driving directions on Yahoo Maps. If you get turned around then call the receptionist. When you're early and no one else is, you have now created an instantly good impression. You look eager and serious. Only a handful of interviewers will feel uneasy that you caught them off guard. But you will not look bad; it's a good thing. This is also a wonderful time to practice. Look over notes on the company you are interviewing with. I highly recommend this. It is of the utmost importance to know history and services of the company you are talking to. You can also use this time to take in surroundings, ask for water, and even go to the bathroom one last time to check your appearance before introducing yourself.

The introduction is not so bad. Be sure to look the interviewer in the eye without staring and smile. Look confident. Say to yourself, this is great! I'm getting to sit down and talk with someone about me. The handshake should always be medium grip. Not too tight or else it looks like you are trying too hard. It's not natural unless you are gripping a bat or you ride bulls. But you can't be Gumby either. Just do your best to match their grip. Practicing with a friend seems dumb but it will help. You will probably just need to do it a couple of times to find your grip. Of course you know not too be nervous nor too serious.

Try to enjoy yourself and have confidence in your story. Take time to observe your surroundings. If you are meeting in that persons office, that's the best. You get a chance to peek into their life and search for commonality. Everyone loves commonality. It's like an aphrodisiac that works. Find one thing in common to talk about during the interview and not exhaust the topic. The interviewer will innately and subconsciously feel good about you. After twenty interviews, they will remember you because they made a connection. This will obviously increase your chances for success.

Whether you are in the interviewer's office or not, you need to try connecting through discovering commonality. This is especially poignant because the interviewer is talking and sharing things with you that interest them, themselves. It's okay, its human nature. So use that knowledge to your advantage. Let them talk as long as possible, ask a good two to four questions and try to retire from the conversation on a high note. This will reinforce the positive feeling about you immensely. It's a subconscious thing that no one can deny. It is like an influence, not a smoke screen. In short the interviewer has now been hit with two subconscious reinforcements about how they feel about you. You not only gained commonality, but you made them like you.

Next you transition back to you and the position while keeping up the good vibe. You can do this in several ways, but I suggest asking them, " So, how long have you been with X company? I'm really excited about the opportunity here". This will help you control the flow of the interview, but be sure to give back quickly. If you don't want to try to control the flow of the interview ask, " I tell you, X Company seems like a fantastic place to work. How long have you been here?" Or, "what do you think about it?"

This will then cause a normal interviewer to think to themselves, "Oh yeah, I need to interview you". They will get back right on track. If they don't, then you can continue letting them talk until it dawns on them. Just lean back a little and smile. If the interviewer is not talking or didn't respond in a way that opened them up, complement them. This is essentially what you are trying to do if they open up and talk to you. "Beautiful kids, boat" etc. "I have always wanted to visit that place (picture they have in the office). I'm jealous; how was it?" You get the idea.

During this time you are also able to observe the interviewer and see how they respond to your questions. This will tell you what type of style to lean towards or adapt for the interview. Always try to gauge the interviewers personality. Try to understand how to reinforce their feelings about you. If an interviewer is light and jovial, then play with them a little bit. Don't be too serious and look as relaxed as possible. Reflect their type of humor. Do they make off color jokes or are they dry? Perhaps they have quirky humor? Whatever the case, do not cross the lines and try to mimic it without being fake. Realize that some interviewers will try to use humor to get you to relax as they set you up on questions. Through your answers they will covertly try to discover who you really are. They will tell more about you through your reactions, versus relying on just your answers.

If the interviewer is very straightforward and business like, then don't ask questions unless they tell you it is okay. Do not get too personal with them. They don't feel comfortable sharing with you. Sit up straight, lean in towards them, look like you are hanging on every word and just agree with them. They like people who see them as smart and really listen when they are talking. Try to be very brief and concise, come prepared to be grilled. No matter how much they seem like they like you, they are trying to slip you up. Do not give in and confess. Hold your ground, have faith in your story and remember they do not know you. Be confident in your answers; make sure they are congruent and consistent.

Now that you have settled in, the probing and grilling session will begin. Take a drink of water, clear your throat and grab the microphone. By the way, if they offer you water take it. It would be ruder if you didn't, plus it helps you to pause so that you may pace yourself. And damn it sure tastes good when you have just taken a bite of the Sahara. Remember this probing session should continue the flow and positive feeling you created. All you have to do is perform your story. Let it rip, but control the pace. Relax, breathe steady and inflect high notes at certain points. This creates a pleasing rhythm to speak with. It is best to be you in the sense of rhythm. Just talk how you would to a great acquaintance. Note an acquaintance; don't act like they are your best friend. You don't want to be trading slang right now or being too chummy. That would either be too real for them or they would not know how to respond. You also don't want to be fake. Be yourself, but relaxed and interested, speaking clearly and concisely.

One of the worst things to do is ramble aimlessly. If you find that you get off track then ask the interviewer a question. Take this time to pause and remember where you are. If you cannot do that, just don't veer off course. No matter how comfortable you feel. Think of doing the interview like showing up and doing a job that you know through and through. Come in, do your work and leave. Make a contribution. Be as productive as possible with your time. Be pleasant and don't disturb anyone or make waves in the system. Fit the mold.

When the interviewer asks you a question no matter how ready you are with the response, never interrupt or cut off the interviewer. You may only ask, " Pardon me, I don't mean to cut you off, but may I ask you something?". If you want to interrupt to make a statement, then say, " Pardon me, I don't mean to be rude, but may I inject something?".

Use this sparingly (one to two times tops) in the interview. Instead, do your best to listen to the complete answer and then pause, giving your response in a steady flowing rhythm. Try to feel your words vibrating as they travel through your throat and out into space. Momentarily pause as if you were asked a question that stumped you. If your previous answers were concise, then fishing around the question or gross elaboration is just fine. You will pass without destroying the vibe. Try not to loose pace and keep the regular pattern of facial expressions. Smile when you normally would and look interested and serious throughout the session. Another great way to go is using the diversion technique. Simply and fluidly transition the conversation on to another topic or ask the interviewer a question.

This should help you figure out how to present yourself and interact with the interviewer. It may all seem a bit foreign, fake and too methodical, but trust me, it will help you. Just take your time and practice. I did it the hard way. I went on a plethora of interviews and paid close attention perfecting my routine and story each time. I also honed my nonverbal communication and reverse probing. I have been on more interviews than most people you know combined. I know these techniques because I have discovered them on all my interviews, real time. You can save yourself the time by rehearsing your story to yourself or to a friend. A little role play baby, but there is no kind of substitute for the real thing. Actual interviews are real time and dynamic. It changes constantly. Styles, what is asked, what is verified, how the process works and what kind of resumes work all change. Role-playing will at least get your first draft story written and rehearsed so you can spread the gospel of you. Begin the evolution of your life.

I'm sure you are chomping at the bit now. You think this is all great Jason, but tell me what the heck do they ask you in the interview? I say read on brothers and sisters.

QUESTIONS THE INTERVIEWER WILL ASK

Compiling a list of every interview question I have been asked or answered is a daunting task that I'll reserve for Big Blue. In the interim, I will share with you the major questions asked in most interviews. The qualifier is that most interviewers asked me these same questions over and over. Sometimes they are asked a different way and certainly a different order. Nonetheless, they are accurate. I will first list out the questions that you may have a quick reference sheet. It would be a fantastic idea to use it in a role- playing. Master these questions with fluidly and rhythm.

Quick Reference Sheet

1. What do you know about us?

2. How did you hear about this position and us?

3. Why are you interested in this position?

4. What don't you like about your current position or company?

5. What do you like about your current position or company?

6. Are you a team player or do you like to work by yourself?

7. Do you have a problem with working in a noisy environment?

8. What motivates you?

9. How long have you been doing what you do now?

10. Tell me about your current position?

11. Do you like your boss/agree with management?

12. May we contact your current employer?

13. What type of processes and or measurements does your company have?

14. What type of measurements do you have for yourself?

15. What makes you think you fit this position?

16. What type of interpersonal skills do you have?

17. What contributions have you made in the past?

18. If I were to talk to your supervisor, what would they say about you?

19. What would you or other people say is your biggest weakness?

20. What would you or other people say is your strongest attribute?

21. Do you embrace technology? How do you feel about using it everyday?

22. Are you from here (this area)?

23. Did you go to school here?

24. Have you ever done this type of work before?

25. What type go management style do you prefer?

26. What type of money do you expect?

27. What do you make now?

28. Tell me about your biggest challenge and how you responded.

29. Tell me about your biggest success in your work or personal life.

30. Tell me about your work history. Give me a recap of your career.

31. Tell me what other skills you have.

32. What are your goals in life? Where do you want to be in five years?

33. What do you hope to achieve in this position and with this company?

34. Explain any gaps in your work history.

35. Explain changes in your career.

36. What did you study in school?

37. Did you put yourself through school?

38. If you moved or going out of state for the job-Why do you want to move here?

39. How do you feel about being separated from everyone you know?

40. Do you have a car, laptop?

41. Did you move here by yourself?

42. What do you do with your free time?

43. If we were to hire you, how much time would you need before you can start?

44. Are you looking at other opportunities?

ANSWERS TO THE INTERVIEWER'S

QUESTIONS

1.   **What do you know about us?**

Be sure to look at the company website for the answers to this one. You want to say at least three things about the company. I would look at the history and mention how long the company has been in business and how profitable they are. Also, look at their core products/services and mission statement. This way, you can align your story by incorporating their mission into your purpose. Lastly, mention something off their brag page. Look at their most recent press release for example. Use this to talk about something they deem as exciting.

2.   **How did you hear about this position and us?**

Try to use some referring person, i.e. recruiter or employee of the company. If you can't say that you were referred then say that you have been interested in working for X company for a while now and that you found the position on their company website. This always sounds better than finding the job on monster or the newspaper.

3. Why are you interested in this position?

Here you need to be specific. Look at the job description on the company website. Talk about how you think it is better than your current job. How it would be more challenging than your current job. You see more of a potential for growth within X Company and you really would like to be apart of them.

4. What don't you like about your current position or company?

You do not find it challenging and do not see any growth opportunity there. Talk about wanting more responsibility. With these types of questions you want to be general as possible. Only give specifics if the interviewer prods you further. It would be safe to talk about being micro managed as long as the position you are interviewing for actually gives you less supervision. You can also flip this around and talk about how you prefer close management style if that's what they offer. Don't talk about money unless you are interviewing for some sales oriented or commission based position. Don't bad mouth your present company, co-workers or boss, no matter what. If the interviewer has some insight or asks you to speak your mind, just talk about how your present company is great but not the right fit for you.

5.   What do you like about your current position or company?

Here, just talk about some genuine things you like. Not really perks, more like management style, hours, co-workers, boss or company values.

6.   Are you a team player or do you like to work by yourself?

If the job you are interviewing for has a team aspect to it. Talk about how you thrive in that kind of environment and how you feel teams are more productive and motivating. You really work well with others and love the interaction. If your job is more independent talk about how working with others slows you down, but you do it and enjoy it when necessary. You prefer to have more control and responsibility, because you are so intrinsically motivated that you always get the job done. You are a goal setter.

7.   Do you have a problem with working in a noisy environment?

This question is another way of asking question number six (are you a team player?). Just answer this the same way. To be brief you can say that noise does not affect you because you have worked in both environments so you just adapt to the environment.

8.   What motivates you?

If you are in sales the there is nothing better than saying money. If finance then say money and helping people develop a plan to accomplish their goals and then seeing them through with them. If you are in anything else then say something about the values of the company found in their mission statement. Or, you could say family and accomplishing your goals.

9.   How long have you been doing what you do?

It is be better to have two years in any profession. If you don't, then say at least one year in your current position. I would not mention any gaps, just run them together.

10.   Tell me about your current position?

Answer this like number five. Also add in specific job duties and details that align with what you said on the resume. Remember to make things sound reasonably better than they are. For example, " I hit all sales goals and customer service metrics. " You could also say you have management or team lead experience over a team of seven to ten versus one or two. Be sure to be as specific as possible here and highlight four to five job duties. Mention if it is a team or individual work you do and paint the appropriate picture.

11.   Do you like your boss/agree with management?

You want to always say "Yes" to this one. You really don't need to express your opinion here even though the interviewer is asking for it. Be positive.

12.   May we contact your current employer?

Definitely say "No". You do not want them to call your current employer because you do not want the interviewer to be able to verify any thing you say.

13.   What type of processes and or measurements does your company have?

Say something about having customer service metrics in place. That seems to be the buzzword these days in business starting with the fortune 500's. If you are in some sort of sales or finance then talk about commission structure monthly goals etc. If you are in any other business then just talk about whatever goals your company has for you.

14.   What type of metrics do you have for yourself?

Here they are probing to see if you are goal oriented and that you set goals for yourself. Talk about learning a new skill such as getting a certain type of license that pertains to the industry that you are in. You can even talk about learning a new language in six months with tapes you bought. You can also use personal family goals or buying a home. Be sure to be specific here and describe whatever your goal is in detail. Anyone can reply with a knee jerk response about having a goal, but any good interviewer will probe to see what that goal is. So, describe it in detail make a visual picture for them.

15. **What makes you think you are a good fit for this position?**

You will be well prepared for this if you viewed their job description, mission statement and brag page on the company website. Just mesh this with your current job duties and responsibilities. Also talk about how it would be more rewarding to you for a reason other than money. Say something about being a team player and enjoying the work and atmosphere. Say how you have experience in the job functions. Be sure to add that you desire to move beyond that position and hope to be able to mentor or help someone else learn the job and become a star like you.

16. **What type of interpersonal skills do you have?**

Here they just want to see that you are a team player and you will talk and get along with others. Without being disruptive. They equally want to know if you can act professionally with clients and/or customers. Therefore you can convey that by saying you enjoy working with others and truly enjoy working with clients. Say you find people intriguing and always learn something from those you interact with.

17.   What contributions have you made in the past?

This is where you need to dig in and find something that set you apart. Whether that was being in charge for a time period, putting out a difficult fire (problem) or proposing some resolution or idea that increased the bottom line or increased productivity. Perhaps you found a more efficient way to do something or helped organize something. You might have helped your team get on top of your volume by putting in extra hours.

18.   If I were to talk to your superior, what would they say about you?

This is another example of why you do not want to allow them call your present employer. Say that your superior finds you a true contribution to the team and will hate to loose you. Furthermore you do not complain when challenges arrive and you are a positive person. Feel free to elaborate more, but be sure to hit these points.

19.   What would you or other people say is your biggest weakness is?

Remember, even though the question is asking for something negative about you. Respond with a positive like, "

I'm to hard on myself", or "I am a pushover for charity", or "I can be too aggressive with attaining my goals or new business."

20.   What would you or other people say is your strongest attribute?

Well here the sky is the limit, there is probably nothing you can say wrong here as long as it is tied to work or success. No pie eating contest or the like. I like to use, "I am a leader and problem solver". You can go in many directions with that one. Try to come up with four or five attributes or qualities about yourself. Such as being a good listener, loyal, patient, smart, likeable and adaptability.

21.   Do you embrace technology? How do you feel about using it everyday?

Respond with a resounding "Yes" then elaborate on whatever software and hardware that you have or currently use. You can further affirm the statement by saying, " I do not know how we could live without it, it's great".

22.   Are you from here (this area)?

This seems like a dumb filler type question. If you are from the area then great, talk about all the people you know in business and all the champions you have in your community. If you are not from the area then they want to see that you have lived in there for at least one year and that you have been busy with activities that put you in front of new people all the time. It could be a church group, bowling, biking, anything. As long as it gets you out into the community.

It is important to talk about how you made so many new friends and you have no plans on moving, that this is where you want to live forever. You are now planting your roots here. You also know that it might take some time to develop new business relationships. You find great success in your natural market selling to anyone you come into contact with. You sell to people you meet at an event or party and anyone that you do business with. Perhaps they installed your cable or you bought tires from them. You get the idea. You will be fine with this question if you are sure to be positive and outgoing and the fact that you love to meet new people and you are not scared to approach them for business.

23.   Did you go to school here?

This is a derivative of number twenty-two. Here it does not matter if you did not go to school in the area. They want to know if you will be able to get to know people in the community and forge new relationships. Answer the same way as above. Sometimes this question will be asked to find common ground. It can only help if the interviewer went to the same school. Be sure to ask them immediately " What school did you go to?" before talking trash or accidentally say something negative about their alma mater.

24.   Have you ever done this type of work before?

I would try to say, "Yes", if you can't then be sure to say that you have done similar work or that you fell as though it is not much of a stretch from your current job. Most of your duties and skills easily transfer over into this position. Be prepared to be specific.

25.   What type go management style do you prefer?

The best thing to do is to find out what kind of style they have there. Ask about it before they ask you or play it safe by saying that you do not have a preference. Say you find you work well without being micro managed but it does not bother you in the least to have a more involved manager, you suppose it could only help. Now if you know for sure that this position is more independent, then talk about how you truly dislike being micro- managed. You just need to be told what you need to get accomplished, and you will get it done attitude is best here.

26.   What type of money do you expect?

Don't be bashful. Be sure that you ask for an amount that is within five thousand of the annual salary. When you talk about commission, if you have been in sales or the industry for two years or more then say at least seventy five thousand for your first year. This would be for a company that says their first years average for new people is sixty thousand, composed of a salary and commission component. If your job only pays a flat salary then ask for five thousand more what you think the salary is. Please do yourself a favor. When you talk numbers here, inflate your present salary by five to ten thousand then ask for more. This way you will definitely come out ahead. They will not look at your tax return and if you tell them they cannot contact your current employer there won't be any way to verify it.

27.   What do you make now?

I answered this one in the previous question, number twenty-six.

28. **Tell my about you biggest challenge and how you responded.**

Try to make this work related. If you can't, that is fine, just be sure that it has elements of dealing with a problem others could not solve. Or something that you had never been confronted with before. You rose to the challenge and overcame you did not panic or quit.For example, " My biggest challenge was moving here without any support system (friends, relatives etc.) and successfully making it happen. I developed a plan and followed it through." For locals to the area then use personal life or death struggles or make it work related. You could use a difficult client no one else could deal with and that client ended up giving you a great review. Perhaps even using a staffing shortfall to your advantage or having to take on more responsibility than you are accustomed to, but you liked it and became stronger for it.

29. **Tell me about your biggest success in work or personal life?**

This is like the previous question, number twenty-eight. Your best response will be a story about overcoming a great obstacle and learning from it while getting stronger. Try to look proactive here as well. You want to look like your successes are goals achieved by your design. For example, "moving to Colorado" or "attaining a series seven license." If you can use family as well, though you better be sure that there are pictures everywhere in the interviewers office indicating that they hold creating a family as the best accomplishment.

30.   Tell me about your work history. Give me a recap of your career.

All right, now it is story time. Be sure to recap your crafted story in the same order and say the same things, just shorten it. Talk about the more pertinent jobs and highlight one to two duties that apply to the current job you are interviewing for. Remember to stay focused and allow questions but keep the pace and flow. You do not want them to trick you up here and throw you off or catch a statement that does not mesh with your resume.

31.   Tell me what other skills you have.

Here you can elaborate on anything you wanted to say but have not been able to find a way to introduce it into the conversation. Brag about yourself some more. I can speed read, I work with charities, and I am a leader by coaching a team or being on some board. You have lots of relationships or business

61

connections around town. Say whatever, but be sure to sprinkle in something specific like you know X program. This way they won't think your getting off track talking about yourself.

32.   What are your goals in life? Where do you want to be in five years?

Did I say story time a minute ago? Now it is time to tell your future story made up of your dreams and probable reality. If you have spent time pondering your life and what you want out of it like I asked you to do earlier in the book, then you will rock this one. If you didn't then just say the following, " I want to be successful in X Company". I want to move up, take on more responsibility and be financially rewarded for it. I want this so I may pursue other outside interests like traveling twice a year starting with Peru and France." Be illustrative; create a visual picture, the more details the better. You could say you want to own a home at X place and you hope to start a family. The interviewer just wants to see that you think ahead and set goals because most people who do are successful. I say elaborate and be illustrative so that they remember you.

33.   What do you hope to achieve in this position and with this company?

You can just reiterate, where you see yourself five years from now with this company. Say, " I want to move up and take on more responsibility and be financially rewarded for it. I also hope to bring some innovation to the company and be able to give back through mentoring and representing the company well outside of work".

34.   Explain any gaps in your work history.

I would not put any gaps on my resume so that you avoid this question. Interviewers do not like gaps. If you must explain it, then I would talk about a family crisis like death. You could say you went back to school or you were attaining a new license and you were studying. One last option is to say that you resigned form your company and were using your reserves while you found another job. This can be sketchy though. This will be a red flag to the interviewer so handle it delicately by saying your manager left and you just were not gelling with new management or new company direction. You can even say that you are dating someone you worked with there and thought it was best that one of you left the company so you did. No matter what you say, it will be better than saying you were laid off.

35.   Explain changes in your career.

This is another red flag to the interviewer especially if you have more than two changes in three years or three changes in five years. The way to flip this to a positive is to say that you have changed your careers because you continually challenge yourself to learn new things and to increase your skill set. Brag about how you always accomplish your goals. You can talk about changes in the industry or seeing the writing on the wall for X Company. Say you were proactive and got into something more challenging. It is okay to add that you would hit all your sales goals but you could not make any more money so you left to go to a higher paying industry.

36.   What did you study in school?

I know this question seems obvious but look closer. If your degree is not the industry norm, then spin it to have cross over appeal. Or you could talk about other courses that you took that are applicable. This will probably not be checked so roll with it. If you were in general studies that goes all over the map just lump in some courses and quickly move to the next question. At this point if you have an interview then they already saw what you studied on your resume so don't sweat it, but there is no need to hang around on the subject either.

37. Did you put yourself through school?

I just so happened to have done this myself. I have inadvertently stumbled across a great thing to brag about that interviewers really like, so use it. Say, "Yes" and at the very least you partially paid for school through scholarships or other jobs. If you can say you paid for your other bills and housing then please do. This shows the interviewer that you set goals and are responsible enough to get it done no matter what it takes.

38. If you moved or going out of state for the job-Why do you want to move here?

Just talk about the state, culture and activities you can do in the new location that you cannot do where you are now. Mention how you visit the area often and have wanted to live there for several years. You could not be happier that you will be there and know you do not plan on leaving. If you are bringing someone then be sure to say that your partner loves it to and feel the same way.

39.   How do you feel about being separated from everyone you know?

I would reply, "It bothers me a little bit. I will miss my friends and family but they all understand that this is good for me and what I want so they are supportive of the move". I also don't have a problem adapting to or learning my surroundings. Plus, I truly enjoy meeting new people and look forward to the opportunity to do so." Bam, done.

40.   Do you have a car, laptop?

"Yes", and, "Yes". You always have transportation no matter what. You have access to a computer and have no problem buying one within the first thirty days of being hired.

41.   Did you move here alone?

If "Yes", then no sweat, just talk about how much you looked forward to this opportunity ands have no plans of leaving. If "no" then talk about how much your partner loves the place, supports you and feels the same way.

42.   What do you do with your free time?

Make sure you talk about things you do that cause interaction with new people and form relationships. At the very

least then talk about active hobbies such as playing sports,
reading, working out, anything other than nothing and TV. The
interviewer wants to see that you are engaging with other people
and have a life outside of work. This shows balance.

**43.   If hired, how much time would you need before you
can start?**

Always say "two weeks". You want to give your
company time to adjust and help them make the transition easier.
You could add that you want a little more reserves before you
leave (i.e. one more paycheck). This is standard and customary.
If the interviewer implies that they want you to start sooner.
Then say, " Well, I will put in two weeks notice, but usually they
just ask the employee to leave that day. I guess they don't want
them to spread the disease (malcontent) if you will."

44.   Are you looking at other opportunities?

Always say, "Yes", to this one. Do not be scared, it will
make the interviewer think you are a rational person and
investigating your options. Be sure to elaborate and say, "I have
an offer from another company (I usually say two companies)
but really enjoyed meeting with you today and learning more
about the opportunity. I feel very strongly about the position

here and hope you feel the same way about me. I would like to make a decision soon and hope we will move forward in the process here together."

At this point during the interview you would have bounced around all of these topics that the previous questions cover. Remember to use the techniques mentioned earlier such as when the interviewer finds something in common with you. Go ahead and tangent off the subject. Embrace it and be agreeable, don't worry about getting through this list. More than likely you will not be asked all these questions by one interviewer in one session. Know that some interviewers will use this only as a prop as they focus on your nonverbal behavior. They try to slip you up or get you off track so they then can study your reaction to questions that you were not prepared for. You handle this by following the methods I have shared already. Practicing your flow and rhythm is key. It does not matter if you are losing it underneath. Outwardly, you appear cool and confident through practicing controlling yourself. The interviewer will be impressed and stop trying so hard to trip you. With interviewers like this it is not always what you say but how you say it.

The rest of the interview questions will be resume and job specific. The resume specific questions will have some general concepts. The interviewer is looking to catch you in some misrepresentation. Essentially they are following the flow and congruency of what you wrote down. Make sure the story you tell meshes exactly. As long as you maintain your rhythm and flow they will believe whatever you say. Again, as long as your story follows your resume. It is extremely important that you do not falter here. This is Simon you're talking, to not Paula Abdul-got it? Be strong and lay out your story.

If your resume is one that has little relevant experience, now is the time to be prepared how to explain the tie in. You need to weave your relevance in. For example, you say you managed people and you are truly a grass cutter. This is where you innocently explain how you view it tying in. "When my boss was negotiating other job contracts, he would look to me to lead the team and be responsible for getting the job done. I would have to coordinate the work and communicate with the team". That's it. You do not have to volunteer any more information. If you are nervous that you will be probed some more, then simply use the divergent technique. For example, either glide into your next job with, "Yes, that was a great job, so after that I went to X job", etc. Or you could stay on the same job and just elaborate with a humorous story about being in charge one day or what you learned being in charge. This depends on the interviewer's style. If jovial, then tell a humorous story. If straightforward, then stick to what you learned.

If you have gaps in your resume, then have a good explanation ready. I would recommend not having gaps. Worry about that once you have won the interview and its time for the Human Resources process (dreaded HR). I will foray into that in the next chapter entitled, <u>Human Resource Process.</u>
If you are bound and determined to talk about your gaps now, I would suggest a tale of school, taking care of family or tragedy. Nothing else can explain laziness or being laid off.

If your jobs or experience was relevant then the interviewer will shift right into the job specific questions. These questions will be the mechanics of your job particular tools and software that you use. Questions about these topics will not get too nitty gritty. Just know what they are and how to use them. Deduce what would apply for this job. The best thing to do is to take someone you know to lunch, who is in that field. I once took my friend's father to lunch when I was eighteen. It was the first business lunch I ever had. I knew him pretty well, but always as my friend's father. I would duck him in the hallways. But this was no reflection on him. He was a super cool guy. You see, he owned an art gallery and I have always wanted to own one. I wanted to know his story. How he got started, how does he run it and what kind of money he makes with it? I had to dance around a lot for that last question.

Bottom line, it does not matter who the person is. Everyone would love to be treated to lunch and have someone be interested in what they do, ask questions to learn about their job and their life. The benefits to you are gargantuan, Godzilla size, screw King Kong he can't breathe fire. By taking a professional to lunch, you are able to not only learn about the job and tools associated with it. These tips will help you win the interview. You have also learned about the life of this job. How it will impact you, what it is really about (information that no interviewer ever tells you), how to be successful at the job, and most importantly, it is right for you? Not to mention you have probably just earned respect from your lunch date and made a new friend. This is an investment in your future. I discovered in my lunch with my friends father.

He did not always have money; he was raised on a plantation as a worker. I can assure you this is tough work, as my grandfather was raised on one as well. My friend's father studied Sociology in school. After school he went on to become a Social Worker. He always had a love of art and was tired of taking his work home with him. Mentally, social work is a very taxing occupation. When you really care about the people you are helping you still care about them after five o'clock p.m. Some situations are so heartbreaking that I commend anyone in this profession. You deserve to be paid more. This is all to say that he followed his dream and opened the gallery, which over time skyrocketed. He is a man did exactly what this book talks about. He Sat down to figure out what he wanted in life and what he was going to have to do to get there. He followed his dream in school and studied what he wanted, then accomplished the goal by getting out of school and practicing it. Notice he did not hide out in school because he was not sure of what to do with his life. Instead he allowed his goals to change. He then created a new plan to start his business and accomplish his new goals. He certainly believed in himself and had the courage and focus to be relentless. These actions and traits enabled him to fulfill his dreams. Just like you can.

Become a master of time by being patient. Steadily work whittle away at your goals. Do not get frustrated thinking they will never materialize. It will happen if you see time as an ally and see goals as process; if you create a strategy and implement it. One day it will indeed take form. But you have put out the effort and have faith that if you keep striving it will come.

At this point in the interview you should have navigated the dreaded sea of questions, implemented the divergent technique, slammed your story down on the table and have presented yourself as knowledgeable about the position and the company. The vibe is obvious at this point, if you prepared and followed through then you probably have a good feeling and so does the interviewer. If you flubbed anywhere, just work on it for next time. Don't worry…all is not lost. Neither is all gained with a good vibe. You still have two more parts to this interview, your questions and the close.

Your questions should be a part of a rehearsal. You always want to ask at least one question. I would recommend having three to four. Ask questions even if you don't think you have any or you know everything about the job. Ask even if you do not want the job. This is your moment to turn the tables and put the interviewer on the spot. Ask away. Just be sure to not cross the line. You will know. Just always play to the conservative side in a question. I sometimes play a game called "Stump the Interviewer". I do this mostly with the interviewer who tries to stump me. Just back off if they start changing colors or get too nervous. The goal here is to project that you are interested and intelligent. You want to ask pertinent questions about the job, benefits, and duties. Do not ask about the money unless the interviewer has asked you how much you make now or if you are in some kind of sales. Sales jobs are all about the money so its natural. It is why you are there, to make money. I have provided a brief list of questions that you would want to ask. These will be general and safe, conservative questions that will not rub anyone the wrong way.

QUESTIONS FOR YOU TO ASK THE INTERVIEWER

1. What does it take to be successful in this position? (Sure fire crowd pleaser).

2. How long have you been with the company?

3. What is the opportunity of advancement based on my performance?

4. When do the benefits kick in?

5. What are the benefits?

6. What are the goals /metrics / measurements of this job?

7. Will I be on a team? If so how many?

8. When do you perceive to fill this position?

9. Do you have any other questions about me/for me?

10. I'm interested in a long-term career. What is the turn over like here?

11. Is it possible to continue my education or study for specific licensing with your sponsorship?

12. What personality traits do you look for in an employee?

13. Last but not least, The Closing question.

The closing question is singled out because of its weight. Finish the game and finish strong by asking for the job. Good interviewers will have this as part of their criteria and measure you against it. In other words, you want them to check off. Yes, he/she did ask a closing question i.e. asking for the business. It is amazing how many people actually don't ask for the job. Whether they are scared, don't want to be rude or seem presumptuous. In the Interview you are selling yourself. So note that all employers/recruiters want you to ask for the business. They want to see that you are confident, excited and eager to get this job. So don't be bashful when closing the deal.

The ultimate closing question may seem uncomfortable or unnatural, but I tell you, it works every time. This is not magical. This is a checkmark in an activity completed and all interviewers will respond in good way, so ask-

"When can I start?" or say "I am very excited about this opportunity, how may we move forward at this point?"

That's all; it is that simple. The reason this works is because one, it asks for the business, you are closing them. Two, it exhibits the qualities of confidence and that you want the job. Three, it catches the interviewer off guard. Some interviewers, especially in sales, have heard this before, but it always makes them smile. Other interviewers either find it humorous or serious and respect the fact you said it. Even the ones that don't know how to respond stare in awe and wonderment. This finishes the interview with a good vibe and lasting feeling about you. Whatever questions they had in their mind about hiring you are now resolved. You have made am impact on them with such a graceful finish.

All you have to do now is shake hands, complement them again, and thank them for their time and the opportunity to learn more about this job. Also say that you look forward to being a part of the team and/or hearing from them soon. End on a high note and hit the door. You could use different closing questions while keeping the response but it needs to meet the same criteria as mine. If not, you are wasting your time. For some variety I suggest, " I feel good about all the information you have shared with me and do not have any other questions, other than when are you looking at filling the position?" Obviously don't ask this earlier before closing if you plan on using it now. You also might try, " So what's the next step in the process? I am definitely interested in moving forward." Both of these work well in a more conservative interview, but convey the same meaning.

After the interview, send a thank you letter. Address it to the interviewer and send it in the mail the very day you interview. This will ensure that the Interviewer receives it two to three days after meeting with you. It will arrive while they are mucking over whom to choose and still remember you. It will reinforce their good feeling about you. Giving the vibe one last spike to pump up some positivity about you. It will help any lingering doubt and provide some differentiation from your competition. The letter needs to reference the job and the interviewer. You thank them for their time and the opportunity to learn more about the position with X Company. It always makes everyone feel good and shows follow-through. I have enclosed and example for you on the following page.

THANK YOU LETTER

Interviewer
Title
Company
Address
City, state, zip

First name of interviewer-

It was indeed a pleasure meeting with you today. I wanted to
thank you for the opportunity to learn more about your company
and the x position.
X Company seems to be very strong and has ample room for
growth. I like your business model and I know that I would
make an outstanding contribution.
Thanks again for your time and consideration. I look forward to
hearing from you soon.

Best regards,

Sign your name

Print your name

NEGOTIATING YOUR PAY AND HIRING

BONUS

So you're done right? Yee haw! Well not if you're brave enough to negotiate. There is nothing worse than selling yourself short. Make a statement; let the interviewers know that you aren't cheap. You are high quality, and that comes with a price. You get what you pay for, right? Just make sure you can follow through on whatever is you say you can do. If you're up to the challenge then by all means go for it. There is no harm in the interviewers mind if try to negotiate. They will either respect you and give you a closer look or they will tell you they there's no chance and they still respect you. It's all about how you approach the negotiation and what you ask for. Of course, it should be within reason, but you can stretch it a little. One technique I employ is starting high, because you can always go lower. Even if they say no, chances are they will to say no to any amount. Again, don't be outlandish. Have some idea of what they pay or offer already. Hopefully the interviewer has already shared it with you. Do it. Ask if the salary is negotiable and if there is a hiring bonus. They will tell you, especially if they really want you. This will ensure your attraction to them. Don't be disillusioned. Their job is to fill the position. They need to so go with whom they feel is the best for the job and their gut guides them. When you attempt to negotiate you are causing them to think,

" Wait a minute. Who is this person talking to? Is another company possibly offering a hiring bonus or a higher salary? All we have are benefits. Well, I like this person but I am not ready to make a decision but I do not want to loose them".

 Whatever the case, the interviewer is getting worried about missing the opportunity of you. They want to make a quality hiring decision. So tread the waters. The real goal of the Interview and this whole book is to make them want you. The negotiation will tell you everything you need to know if you need a gauge for the job, in order to understand if they want you for the position.

To ease into the negotiations is important to be gentle. You can open up the topic by saying, " May I ask you a question? In you career here, have you noticed if they pay a signing bonus, if so, how often?" You could be a bit more straightforward and say " Is the salary negotiable?" but do this with the least amount of abrasive as possible using your tone. This is a safe way to enter the topic. If you get pushback or a negative look and/or response, then simply say" I'm sorry, I was only concerned because I am interviewing with a few other companies and just want to make sure I have a all the information I can to make a sound decision."

They won't say a word to that. If the Interviewer responds I am positive way, you are in like Flynn, and make a move. You can either collect the information from the interviewer first and then ask what the numbers are, or you can charge right in with what you want. I would suggest letting the interviewer tell you because you have already prompted him at this point.

Everything should be going great by now. You know they want you, and you have an opportunity to create your salary and make some money on this deal. Don't blow it. This is when steady rhythm and controlled nonverbal behavior is extremely important. Think cool, not James Dean but Robert Deniro-controlled, serious, but real and genuine. Don't get too excited, but don't seem too interested either. Gently go back and forth like Ping-Pong except make it a short game. You don't want this to go more than two counter offers on your behalf. I would suggest only going back one time with one counter offer and sticking firm to it. You may not make not the most money this way, but you don't turn this into a bazaar and piss on the interviewer. This needs to be win/win with the interviewer thinking they have the upper hand, ensuring the likelihood of the deal. I would normally not ask for more than 35% higher than what they are offering. Sometimes I would ask for 100% more if I had another job lined up. That is why I am suggesting the 35%. It's a safe bet for your odds. The most solid bet though would be 15%. I would say go with no more than 20% higher and it is still safe. If you don't want to risk anything then this is your betting limit.

One brief, noteworthy technique is to never accept the job right away, always ask if you can get back with them in one to three days. If they ask why, say, " I have other interviews set up and it would be wrong to not follow through". You can also say, "I have been offered another job and need some real time to think about it, so that I'm 100% sure of the decision." This will do two things besides making them salivate. It will improve your negotiations and win the interviewer over to your side, which will be of great help in the human resources process. If negotiating may seem too ballsy or you don't want risk loosing the opportunity don't do it. Just realize that it is extremely rare for someone to offered a job and take it away if you ask for a couple of days to think about. How did you do? I hope better than what you thought, or at least you are better able to gauge their interest in you. Well done, I'm proud of you. You got guts kid. There you have it. You are through. Take a breath and have beer to get warmed up to the last phase, the Human resources process. Or want I like to call Celebrity Poker This is where the gremlins go to work to disprove everything you have said and written. Don't worry; you can handle it with this next chapter.

THE HUMAN RESOURCE PROCESS OR CELEBRITY POKER

This is the last leg of the race and you are in the lead. If you can hang on victory is yours. If you get squeamish, then you will lose and waste an opportunity. Don't worry there will be others. If you want to win, listen up. What I am going to share with you about the human resources process is how to make the system work for you. I will also share some techniques you can use to ensure that the HR people discover what you want them too, not what you don't.

The human resource process usually takes between one to two weeks. Generally it depends on the protocol of the company. Occasionally the process goes longer than this time frame, usually indicating there is a problem. Either they are looking at another candidate at the last minute or they are freezing the hiring process.

I feel that it necessary to explain the job let down technique. Now it's time to shift back to the fundamentals of the human resource process. There are a few key elements to the human resources process. You will find these common across all HR departments. There's some give and take, some are more thorough than others. Some can be bypassed if the interviewer or manager really wants you.

85

The major elements of the human resource process are: application, resume verification, reference calling, criminal background check, credit check and miscellaneous tests. Applications always irritate you, because you have already written a resume and sent it in. You might have to reenter your information on the hiring company website. It sucks, but you've got to do it again. At least you probably have the job now. Remember to make it exactly like your resume. In fact, it is a good idea to keep your resume with you and just pull it out to begin transcribing. It will make you look better, prepared and not forgetful.

There will be other parts to the application. Usually there will be standard forms for background, criminal and drug checks that you must read and agree to sign. Not all employers do all checks, but I would always be prepared. You would hate to loose it here. There will be other company specific forms to read and sign along with emergency contacts and references. Have your previous companies phone numbers and addresses handy and know your former supervisors names. If you have trouble with any of your history, or think your story might be interpreted differently if someone else told it, then just keep the information handy but don't write it down. Let the HR department do the legwork. You won't look too bad, but only withhold this information if you must.

The more complicated part to the application lies in the questionnaire/survey portion. Here you must be sure to not mark "Yes" for "May we contact your current employer?". This way they will not verify anything with them. This is a powerful tool. Also do not ever mark "Yes" to "Have you ever been released from a prior job?" There are many variations on this question. Point is, if you were let go do not mention it. Have a great story and cover up the details. Remember that when they call, human resources are not allowed to say you were fired. The HR from the company you are interviewing with can only ask " Would you rehire this person?" So hedge your bets on this one. The rest of the questioning is straightforward. You can figure out what they are asking so do yourself favor paint a solid picture of yourself. You weren't late, didn't steal, have no bad credit or criminal records. If they find something on your criminal record then say, " I thought that it was expunged as it was supposed to be. I'm sorry I certainly wasn't aware of this". If they will find bad credit then say, "Yes" to a problem and explain that you have worked a payment plan out in the past with a creditor. Ask for a copy of the credit report being looked at so you will know exactly what you will need to dispute.

Otherwise you don't know what you really need to take care of. There are three major credit bureaus and most companies just choose one to pull credit from. Therefore you can have different information on different bureaus. When you are asked why you left a job, say something to the effect of "I wanted to pursue a career in X". Perhaps you left to for a higher position or because of a quality of life change such as moving. It looks best to say that you are currently employed on the application. Which can be tricky to navigate but these techniques will help. If you do employ these techniques you are taking responsibility for the outcome of the situation. I can only tell you that I have seen it work again and again.

Resume verification is always a doozy. Recall what I said a moment a go. It seems that the best thing to do on the application is to mark, "No don't contact my current employer". I have actually asked many people who work in HR about this question. When I first started interviewing, I did not know if it was bad to mark "No", like something you were hiding. In reality this is not the case. It is perfectly acceptable to mark "No". HR regards this as you not wanting to rock the boat at your current job until you are officially hired at this job. If you are not working and/or were fired, this is your savior. If you mark, "No", HR cannot contact your current employer whomever that is. They will not be able to call and verify if you still work for that company or not. This means you do not have to answer the question " Were you ever un-willfully terminated from a position", and present yourself as still working. The last perk third that you can say whatever you want about your current job during the interview. No one will verify anything about it. This is a trump card. Use it and abuse it. It works every time.

It is customary for HR to look back two to three jobs. I say this is customary, but there are some HR departments that research every job except the current job you marked, "No do not contact". What you need to do is listen to what holes they find in your resume. If they verify the dates of employment, which most HR do, and you have a gap then try to explain why. Say that you went back to school, were working another non-relevant job, or that you were working for yourself. Or someone else claim that you were 1099, essentially meanings you are subcontracted and not salaried. These could be positions were you a re learning a trade. If you use a non-relevant job then have a buddy be the boss at a real location. When HR calls your previous jobs they are not only looking at tenure dates, but they will verify your job title as well. They will not verify how much you get paid. They will dance around whether you were fired, if they are that hardcore, but usually they don't ask because the company you left is not supposed to tell them. They don't really verify your job function thoroughly, which is why your story and resume can have some spicy additions. If they weasel a moment with your prior supervisor they can find out more on your job function and what they thought about you as an employee. If your manager is on your side then you should have spoken to them about how they would respond already. If you have not spoken to them or don't know what they will say then take them to lunch to find out, just to play safe. If your manager is not on your side, then hopefully they will not elaborate too much. HR will only ask, "Would you rehire this person?". All they can say is "Yes" or "No".

As far as degrees and education goes, very rarely are you asked to provide a transcript. So I would not be concerned about this. Neither would I be concerned about graduate assistantship or other internships. They are easy to work with and on your side willing to help you. Just call and tell them what you need.

Licensing will be verified if they can access a database or make a phone call. I would not play around with licenses. If they are relevant to the job then they will be verified, no "ifs", "ands" or "buts" about it.

If you are self-employed put your personal phone number for work number of your previous supervisor. Don't bother with obtaining an HR number. This allows you to control your tenure. Just make it match the resume. Also, if you are in a financial industry then you have a tracking form called the U5. You cannot deny this information reported. It would be a good idea to get a U5 yourself. So that you can see what others are seeing and make it match your resume, tenures and your story that you tell. I would advise anyone to be proactive and protect him or herself by always submitting a resignation before quitting. If you are getting fired then ask to have them report you as leaving "Voluntarily". This will show up on the U5 and if it is reported as "Involuntary" you are more than likely screwed. Be sure to notice your tenure dates as well and be able to explain any gaps. Know that there is nothing wrong with saying you resigned. Just paint a picture like " I did not want to take advantage of the situation or the company. I did not think it was fair to keep taking their money and they agreed that it would not be of much good for me to stick around another few weeks." I always like to add, "I don't think they want me to spread the disease." You will usually get a chuckle out of that one unless they don't understand what you mean. This is also a good technique to use when you want to say that you can start next week or ASAP.

Even though you might unemployed, if you tell them " I will of course put in the customary two week notice. But my company will want me to leave that day. They don't want me to spread the disease".

Regarding the background check, there is not a whole lot to do here. Unless you have moved around bit and it's hard or pin down information about you or if you have court information that was expunged, then it's pretty straightforward. You know what you are up against here if you have issues. You might want to triple stack the jobs in your case. Also, many employers don't do a very thorough search. They might only search the county you currently live in and the one the job is located in. To help ensure this, on the application I would only put down the last two years of your residency. So don't loose heart the fight not over yet. Think "Cinderella Man" the movie. If you have not seen it then know that it is about a boxer desperate to take care of his family and being relentless in the pursuit of his goal.

Oh lord, the credit check. This one is a breeze if you do not have any bankruptcies, foreclosures, collections, judgments or liens. If you have at least three open trade-lines (i.e. a car, credit cards, home and installment loans) without being late then you are gold and probably have a high credit score. If you don't have this type of credit, then we need to talk about strategy.

It is most important not to have bankruptcies and collections. If you do, there is hope by having documentation or a letter of explanation from you on how a catastrophe, death, or sickness took place to cause this situation. You will be all right if your other accounts still open are current. If they are not then good luck and hope that the hiring manger is on your side and wants you badly.

A technique you could employ here is to dispute all the bad items on your credit report and leave the burden of proof on the credit bureau. Now this is especially poignant in a hiring situation where they are relying heavily on your credit. This gives you an out because time is on your side. Order a credit report from all three bureaus. Do it over the phone and have it come through the mail. This will take more time. It will take a minimum of a week to receive the information but probably closer to two weeks. Once you get it, then send a letter back disputing all the bad information. Say it's not yours and sit back. It usually takes a month for you to get a letter back that says they received your request and will look into it. Then it usually takes another month to get a reply. Now you must act surprised and tell the company, "Gee this dispute process looks like it will take some time. I don't know if I can wait that long, isn't there something we can do?" This works wonders.

The hiring manager should be on your side. They want you. You told them you have other opportunities but really want this job. You have done everything else right and hopefully everything else checks out. The deal is, they don't want to take the risk in loosing you, nor have to spend more time trying to find another candidate. They will work for you and be your advocate. If they have weight in the company, they might get your credit issue waived. Now the pressure is going to be on you hardcore at the job, and you better be able to follow through.

The way to respond to an awkward credit situation when it is first brought to your attention is to say, "That it is not mine, I don't know what that is". Or " I am disputing that right now." If you go with option one then they will ask for proof of the dispute and when you disputed it. If you go with option two then you need information from the collectors. If you got it, you are gold. If not, just call and set a payment plan. Get it faxed to you and send it to HR stating that you are current on this account and this is your settlement. Do not mark, "Yes" " I have worked out a payment with a company in the past". Leave it blank unless you know what type of loan and company it is. If asked, just say credit cards. Then discover whom the debt is with and work it out. This will get you through the process and get you the job.

Actually following through is up to you. I say you might as well

take care of it so it does not continue to haunt you.

TYPES OF TESTS YOU MIGHT HAVE TO TAKE

The next element of the HR process is the testing. This usually falls into three types, which are either combined or used all together at the same time depending on the company. These categories are: personality, job knowledge, and general skills.

The personality tests are probably the most overweighed and misunderstood type of tests. They also give you the hardest time trying to figure out how to answer. I have a back ground in Psychology, which taught me how to interpret what the test is asking for. The Personality test is supposed to determine what motivates you and how you respond to stimulus. The employer uses this to gauge if you will be a reliable employee and what type of position would best suit you. Now come on, we all may struggle with different learning issues, but we can still overcome them with hard work, focus, and most of all relentlessness. Yes, we may all have a propensity for certain jobs, but that does not mean we should not be allowed to pursue other jobs. I find people in careers with fierce dedication had to fight to get there. They want it more and worked harder to overcome obstacles more than the next guy. That is to say, our jobs and opportunities should not be predetermined for us. The current testing used to pigeonhole everyone is ineffective. Don't buy into it.

The tests can be understood if you first understand your job function. In other words do not be soul searching on theses tests. Answer the questions like it's a regular test in school. There are certain answer that will give you an "A" and other that won't. Also remember that in school you had different subjects, which means you had different answers that would give you "A's" in different classes. Apply that concept to these personality tests. Know the subject for each different type of job you take. Then you can be that person on that test.

Understand that these tests are not as concerned with your moral fiber but instead, your effectiveness at a job. This is especially true if you are going into any type of sales or finance position. Companies don't care if you give blood at the Red Cross. They care if you can convince people to give you their money. These type of companies are looking for answers that on the personality test that say you are motivated by money, you can work independently, you like to take charge, you like to talk in front of groups and you like to socialize. If you answer these test with the previous concepts in mind. You will answer beautifully and probably get the job for finance and sales.

Backing up a bit, you need to know what type of person this company hires or at least an idea of the type of person than applies for that job. The easiest way to discover this is during the interview, when you have an opportunity to ask questions. I would ask, " What type of personality traits does your company look for in a employee?" If you cannot ask this or do not get a clear response, just remember this is not confession. Think about what would be the most effective answer to the question. It will tell you what they are looking for. Be careful to always answer the same type questions the same way. Watch the pattern of the questioning. These tests are designed to trick you and have you answer inconsistently. They are trying to fool you by acting like they are asking a different question when it is really the same question. Be aware and pay attention; don't agonize over how to answer. Just pick what you think is an effective personality for the position and consistently answer the questions that way. Remember, you want to give the right answers, not go to confession.

The Job knowledge test is used more often when the type of job you are getting requires a license. The company needs to be sure that you can still pass a test for license if need be. They do not want train you and spend the money if you're not capable of passing the license exams. Other companies might employ this type of testing, but again it is seldom.

Do your homework for the job knowledge and answer as many questions as possible for the tests. You are told not to worry about answering all the questions. No one ever finishes…just do what you can. Now what this means is that they want to see how many problems you get right vs. how many you attempt. I say increase your odds. The more questions you attempt the higher your percentage will be. The questions are weighted more heavily if there is less to consider. Certainly, don't take this too far and rush to get all the way through. Don't end up with ten questions either. Fact is, you are bound to miss some of the questions. That is what the test is designed for. Don't feel bad if you don't know the answer, just move on, it will wash out.

The third testing component is a general job skills test. These test are going to be the easiest out of the bunch. Different companies use different variations and test for specific skills. You might have a test on how many words you type a minute. There are two variations to this test. Sometimes there will be someone standing over your shoulder, watching you. Otherwise, you are by yourself. If someone watches you, clear your mind, don't look surprised and just focus on the task. Forget about them, they are just watching you do what you do. They are really only applying a little pressure to scare you and test your focus. So stay focused.

The typing part of the test will usually have you look at a page or paragraph and type what you see in a certain amount of time, usually one to five minutes. Your goal should be top type forty words per minute. That's not stellar, just passing. If you cannot do this then remain calm, concentrate and try to be sure that most of the words are correct. The test is designed to see how many words you attempt and how many you get correct. Again, you are told don't worry about getting it exactly right or getting through the whole page. Don't believe that. Keep a steady flow and a balance between the time you spend on making the word correct and getting through at least 35% of the page. Don't try to go back and correct. Try to get all the way through the paragraph with few mistakes. If you are still concerned about this test just practice on a P. C. Time yourself starting at six minutes then get down to five minutes, while continuing to work your way down to one minute. Then practice two times in front of someone who will write a paragraph for you to transcribe. Be sure to change the bold, capitalize and underline, using quotes commas semicolons hyphens and numbers.

In addition to this transcription-typing test you might be asked a question such as, "Why do you think you are the right person for this job?" It could be many other things but this is a common one. Next you will have to type a response, immediately without much time; less in than forty minutes. This test is designed to see how fast you answer on you feet and if you can respond to emails or client questions as well. Its not so much about what your answer is, but it definitely helps to say something professional yet memorable.

Another type of general skills test is eight keys that is usually tested if the position has to do with inventory. Otherwise you don't see this test.

This is a good time to mention job stacking, always have aback up in case the primary job you are interested falls through. I am a firm believer in this because you never know what's going on behind closed doors. What if the company you want to work for says "Yeah, we want you pending the background check and taking X tests" and you are unable to pass the test. It does not matter how bad they want you and if you don't want any other job. Sometimes things don't work out such as a hiring freeze. Therefore the only way to insulate yourself is to have another job on the back burner. Also, this is a great for negotiations because you have someone to measure this company against. You will feel more confident. Not over confident, just confident. This gives you wiggle room and allows you to play a little bit. This would be a good time to experiment with different questions, responses, and push further in negotiations.

Now this is not an easy to create as it sounds. Obviously you must go to another interview and land another job. The tricky part is not ruining a relationship when you don't take the back up job. You never want to burn bridges in business. You may need this job in the future or meet that interviewer in a different landscape. The way to handle not accepting the job is to mention during the interview that you are looking at another company. Say you have been offered the job but you feel that X company is a better fit because xyz. I would say something like, "They will pay you more money, have better benefits for your sick kid, a faster career development. Or it's something you always wanted to learn or do". This way it will not come as a complete surprise and make them want you more. Next, give them the opportunity to counter-offer or go straight to the breakup. Tell them, " Company X is a great company, I would feel good about working here. But right now in my career I feel this is the best option for me. I want to be 100% not 90% sure about the job with you. I don't want to waste your time and money if in three months I have regrets and want to leave. I certainly would hope that we could connect in the future and the position would be open to me if it were still available. I have enjoyed getting to know you hope I don't burn any bridges and that you understand my dilemma."

During this letdown you must appear genuinely heartfelt, that this was a painfully difficult decision. Your goal is to leave the door open in case you change your mind. Be sure to compliment the interviewer, the job, the company and the people you have met so far. You think the world of this place. Wish the interviewer well and thank them again for their time and interest. It means a lot to you, and go on about your way.

FINAL THOUGHTS; GO GET 'EM

Well Damnation. It's done. I mean it. This is how you get a job faster and learn the art of getting a job. I want to congratulate you for your efforts and wish you the best of luck. I know that in time you to will be a great master who gets whatever job you want. You will have this process down pat and nail it every time. Have no fear. Teach others to increase their opportunities and to get the job they want. Help them gain the momentum to charge ahead through life to end up where the envisioned.

"Namaste" my friends. I leave you with some poignant quotes to help you push forward through any obstacles you face and to anyone who tells you cannot do it.

"Success is moving from failure to failure without losing heart"

Winston Churchill

"The past is a foreign country. People do things differently there."   anonymous

"Make time a process, design your journey, be relentless and life will unfold to you."   Jason LeBlanc

Author Biography

Jason LeBlanc, 32 years old. Graduated Louisiana State University in 2000. Majored in Psychology Sociology and English. Currently Holds Series 6, 7, 66 financial licenses. Also holds Life Insurance, Health and Accident Insurance license, Variable Annuity license and former owner of a Mortgage Company in Houston Texas. Now a practicing Variable Annuity Broker Dealer Specialist.

I have had a job since I was 12 years old working at my local pool. I sent my self around the world to play soccer from Russia to Costa Rica. I financed the trips by selling chocolate bars for a dollar. This taught me to be an excellent salesman. Late in life, I put myself through college carrying 5 jobs at any given time. My duties varied from bartending to serving subpoenas while working as a court researcher. I also worked manual labor jobs building above ground pools and ran a real estate sign installation business. These are just a few of the jobs I carried over the years. I worked more than I went to school.

Upon graduating I moved to Houston where I dreamed of working for myself. I entered the work force by interviewing about 20 to 30 times a week for one month. I learned from interviewing in this competitive and fast paced environment. As I moved forward I opened my own mortgage company by convincing the owner to give me a shot though I lacked the mandatory two years experience. I succeeded.

I shut the doors of the mortgage business in 2004 before the national mortgage crisis. I found a company who would relocate me Colorado and pay me for it. I always dreamed of moving to Colorado, a place I would drive 24 hours to from Louisiana to camp hike, bike and rock climb. After a short time I decided to fulfill another goal, a career in financial planning. I completed my Series 6 & 7 in 2005. I truly enjoy my work because I help people envision their dreams and create achievable goals. I coach them along the way and develop personal and realistic strategies. I treat the readers of my book in the same way; I want them to succeed.

I currently live in Colorado with my wife Heather and our dog Yeti. Together we live a balanced life of work and play, as it should be. We Wish you well my friends and good luck.

www.ingramcontent.com/pod-product-compliance
Lightning Source LLC
Chambersburg PA
CBHW032011190326
41520CB00007B/430